Leonardo B. Dal Maso

VILLA BORGHESE AND THE GALLERY

D. EDI. T. s.r.l.
DISTRIBUZIONE EDIZIONI TURISTICHE
Via Antonio Silvani, 90/92
00139 ROMA - Tel. 8120245 - 8122738

Edito e stampato dalla

Narni - Terni

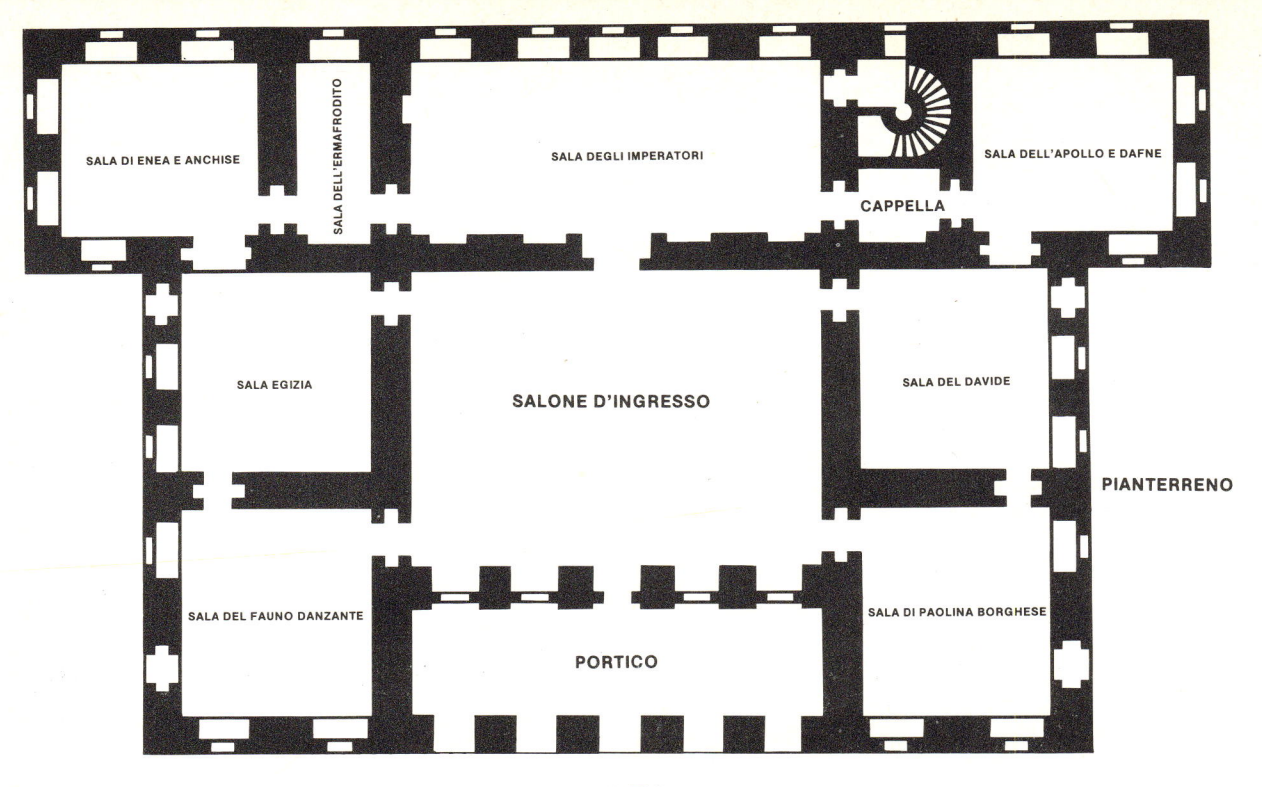

PIANTERRENO

- SALA DI ENEA E ANCHISE
- SALA DELL'ERMAFRODITO
- SALA DEGLI IMPERATORI
- CAPPELLA
- SALA DELL'APOLLO E DAFNE
- SALA EGIZIA
- SALONE D'INGRESSO
- SALA DEL DAVIDE
- SALA DEL FAUNO DANZANTE
- PORTICO
- SALA DI PAOLINA BORGHESE

INDEX

VILLA BORGHESE AND THE GALLERY	3
CLASSICAL MOSAICS AND SCULPTURE	9
BAROQUE AND NEOCLASSICAL SCULPTURE	13
RENAISSANCE PAINTINGS	25
BAROQUE PAINTINGS	47
THE MARBLES	59
INDEX	63

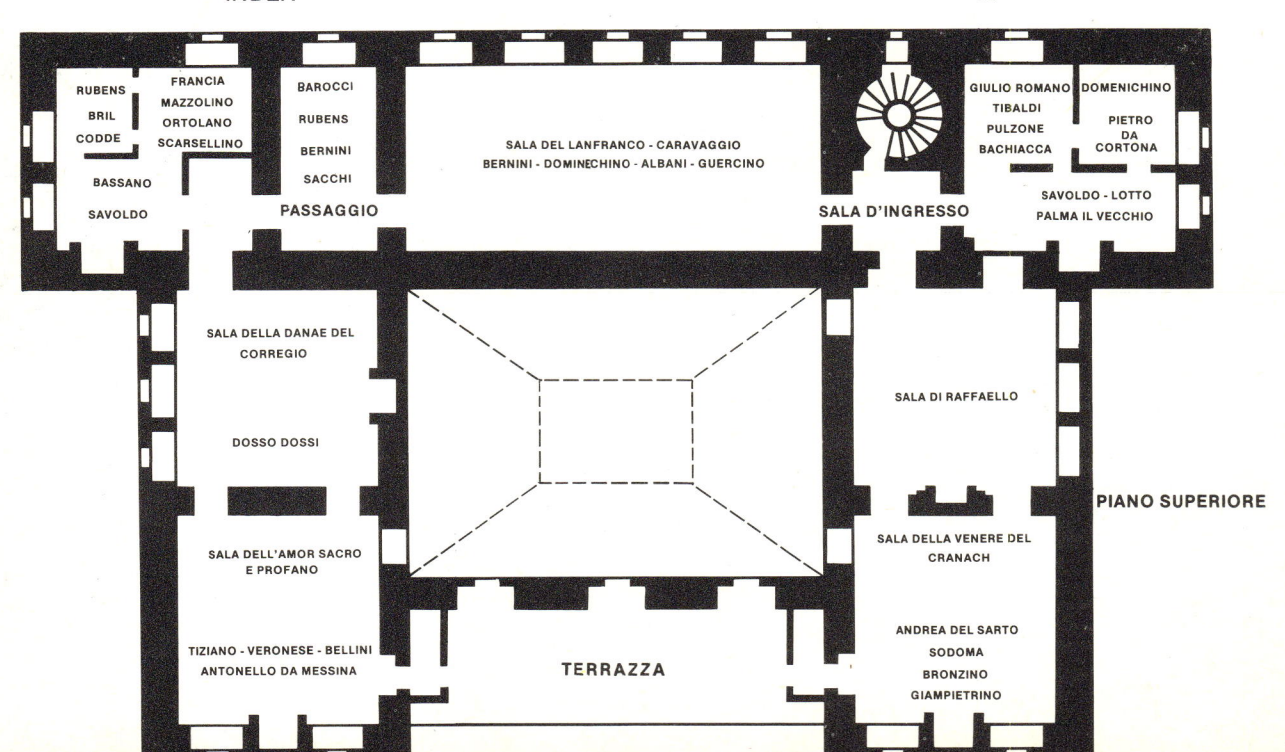

PIANO SUPERIORE

- RUBENS, BRIL, CODDE
- FRANCIA, MAZZOLINO, ORTOLANO, SCARSELLINO
- BAROCCI, RUBENS, BERNINI, SACCHI
- PASSAGGIO
- SALA DEL LANFRANCO - CARAVAGGIO
- BERNINI - DOMINECHINO - ALBANI - GUERCINO
- SALA D'INGRESSO
- GIULIO ROMANO, TIBALDI, PULZONE, BACHIACCA
- DOMENICHINO, PIETRO DA CORTONA
- BASSANO, SAVOLDO
- SAVOLDO - LOTTO, PALMA IL VECCHIO
- SALA DELLA DANAE DEL CORREGIO
- DOSSO DOSSI
- SALA DI RAFFAELLO
- SALA DELL'AMOR SACRO E PROFANO
- SALA DELLA VENERE DEL CRANACH
- TIZIANO - VERONESE - BELLINI, ANTONELLO DA MESSINA
- TERRAZZA
- ANDREA DEL SARTO, SODOMA, BRONZINO, GIAMPIETRINO

VILLA BORGHESE AND THE GALLERY

Scipione Caffarelli, nephew of Pope Paul V, took the name and coat-of-arms of the Borghese family and was made a Cardinal in 1605. The instigator of major public works and famed for his munificence, he was also a skilful diplomat and won the friendship of distinguished foreign personages. In 1602 Tommaso d'Avalos d'Aquino, on hearing that he intended to build himself a villa, gave him the tract of land that lies between Porta Pinciana and Via Flaminia. It is here that the Villa Borghese and its park lie today.

A worthy successor of the Humanists of the Renaissance, Cardinal Scipione devoted himself to literature and the arts, expending huge sums of money on the purchase of ancient sculpture and masterpieces of contemporary painting. It appears that he was so anxious to obtain the classical statue of the Hermaphrodite that he had the facade of the church of S. Maria della Vittoria rebuilt at his own expense. The Casino Borghese was built between 1613 and 1616, mainly for the purpose of housing his collection of ancient and modern sculpture. It was designed by the Dutch architect Ivan van Santen, known in Italy as Vasanzio. The paintings however remained in the huge family palazzo in the Campo Marzio.

During the three centuries that followed the park was embellished by the descendants of Scipione Borghese, who availed themselves of the services of a number of architects and sculptors. In the 17th century separate pavillons were built - the Uccelliera, the Casino della Meridiana and the Fortezzuola. The last-named, which eventually became the residence of the sculptor Pietro Canonica (d. 1959), now houses the Museo Canonica. At the end of the 18th century the whole Villa was renovated in keeping with the taste of the period, and fountains and little temples were built. These include the Fountain of Venus in the garden of the same name behind the Casino and the Fountain of the Seahorses (1791) by Cristoforo Unterberger, the circular temple

The propyleae at the Piazzale Flaminio entrance, by Luigi Canina (1829).

The Fountain of Aesculapius, by Antonio Asprucci (end of 18th century).

was renamed after King Umberto I. It continued to be known by this name for several decades. A driveway and the Avenue of the Magnolias connected it with the Pincio Gardens, which also contained numerous fountains and pavilions. In 1911 the Zoological Gardens were laid out in a seven-hectar area on its autskirts, and in the area to the north of the park were built the Gallery of Modern Art and a number of foreign Academies. The hippodrome in Piazza di Siena became the scene of show-jumping competitions and military parades, and the avenues were still further embellished with monuments given to the city or erected in memory of foreign men of letters who extolled the beauties of Rome in their writings. The first of these was the monument to Goethe in 1902. Then came the one set up by the French in honour of Victor Hugo and the monuments to the Albanian poet Firdusi, J. A. Artigas, hero of the Uruguay war of independence, F. Santander, given by Colombia, and Lord Byron, a copy of a statue by Thorwaldsen. Other statues are of purely Italian interest, such as that of the Alpino of Diana (1791), the fake ruins of the Temple

Cristoforo Unterberger: Fountain of the Seahorses (1791).

of Faustina (1792), the Temple of Aesculapius in the Garden of the Lake (1786), designed by the architect Antonio Asprucci, who also built the ceremonial entrance adorned with the Borghese eagles (1790), which previously stood at the Muro Torto and were subsequently placed opposite the Porta Pinciana.

At the beginning of the 19th century the architect Luigi Canina, the neoclassical restorer of Via Appia, built the propylaea at the Piazzale Flaminio entrance, the so-called Porta Egizia and the Fountain of Aesculapius. After 1874 four grotesque masks and four tritons by Giacomo della Porta (1572) were placed in the Garden of the Lake. They were taken from the Fountain of the Moor in Piazza Navona, and were replaced there by copies. With these embellishments Villa Borghese became the most sumptuous villa and park in Rome; only Villa Doria Pamphili exceeded it in the extent of its parkland. However, unlike all the other Roman villas, Villa Borghese was thrown open to the public by its generous owners.

In 1902 the Villa and the Gallery became the property of the Italian nation, and the Villa

Temple of Aesculapius (1787) by Mario Asprucci, in the Garden of the Lake.

and the Mule, by Canonica, and the equestrian statue of King Umberto I by Calandra and Rubino. The perimeter of the park today measures six kilometres. Very little still remains of the villa built for Scipione Borghese by Vasanzio, apart from the four small rooms on the top floor. In about the middle of the 18th century Marc'Antonio Borghese commisisoned the architect Antonio Asprucci to decorate the rooms; with him worked a host of Italian and foreign stucco-workers, sculptors and painters. The most important of these was Mariano Rossi, who painted the frescoes with the story of Furius Camillus. The Tuscan artists Marchetti and De Angelis decorated other rooms on the ground floor.

On the first floor the big loggia painted by Giovanni Lanfranco (1542-1568 *) was closed in and turned into a reception room; the pictures previously kept in Palazzo Borghese were then moved to this new gallery.

The result was a superb collection which may still today be considered the finest private collection in the world, in spite of the impoverishment to which it was subjected at the beginning of the 19th century at the hands of Camillo Borghese, husband of Pauline Bonaparte. He sold many of the pictures, including that of St. Catherine by Raphael and the Supper at Emmaus by Caravaggio, and he also exchanged two hundred ancient sculptures, including the so-called Gladiator, Mars and the Hermaphrodite, for the estate of Leucadio in Piedmont. These now form the « Borghese Collection » in the Louvre. The impairment caused to the Gallery by Camillo Borghese was partly compensated for by the famous sculpture of his wife as Venus by Canova, and by the archaeological finds that Francesco Borghese had brought from Tusculum by Canina. These included sculpture and the superb mosaics with scenes of gladiators and hunting which were set into the floor of the entrance hall. A few more items were added to the Borghese collection by the Italian state - Savoldo's painting of Tobias and the Angel, two busts of Scipione Borghese and a sketch for the equestrian statue of Louis XIV, which complete the greatest collection in existence of sculpture by Bernini.

Statue of Byron (1959), a copy of the one by Thorwaldsen.

Equestrian statue of Umberto I by Calandra and Rubino (1923).

Statue of Goethe by Gustavo Eberlein (1902-4).

▲ The Aviaries by Girolamo Rainaldi (1617-19). ▼ Main facade of the Casino Borghese.

CLASSICAL MOSAICS AND SCULPTURE

The collection of classical works of art arranged in the ground-floor rooms is extremely interesting, in spite of the severe blow inflicted on it by Camillo Borghese in selling over two hundred sculptures to France. Today, partly due to the acquisition of new archaeological finds, especially from Tusculum, there are 254 antique sculptures in the Borghese Museum. Some of them are of great value, such as the statue of a young girl wearing a peplum, which the majority of experts consider to be an original work of archaic Peloponnesian art. The lively Dancing Satyr is a Roman copy in marble of a bronze statue of the school of Lysippus; unfortunately ill-judged restoration on the part of Thorwaldsen has altered the position of the arms, which perhaps been held together to play the double flute. One of the finest sculptures in Scipione

◀ **Borghese Museum, Hall of the Emperors (end of 18th century).**

Statue of a girl wearing a Peplum, an original work of archaic Peloponnesian art. Room VII.

Dancing Satyr, a Roman copy of an original bronze of the school of Lysippus. Room VII.

10

11 ◀ Statue of a boy on a dolphin, of the period of Hadrian (2nd century A. D.). Room VII.

The wall of the first room. In the foreground, Leda and the Swan, a Roman work which was almost completely restored in the 19th century.

Borghese's collection was the Sleeping Hermaphrodite, brought to light during excavations for the foundations of the church of S. Maria della Vittoria, a Roman copy of a famous Hellenistic work. This statue, for which Bernini sculpted a marble couch resting on an inlaid walnut chest, is now in the Louvre, but it has been replaced by another copy of the same subject, though of a later date and artistically inferior. The mattress, the head and other parts of the body are the result of restoration carried out in the 18th century by Andrea

Mosaic with scenes of gladiators fighting, from Terra nuova near Tusculum (3rd-4th centuries). Entrance room.

Bergondi.
Other outstanding sculptures are that of Leda and the Swan in the first room, extensively restored in the 19th century, and the statue of a boy riding a dolphin which stands in the middle of Room VII. This dates from the time of Hadrian, and probably formed part of the ornamentation of a fountain. The head is not the original one.
One of the finest of the many sarcophagi is that dating from the time of Antoninus (2nd century A.D.). In the spaces between a row of superb Corinthian columns are sculpted the Labours of Hercules. Around the base runs a beautiful bas-relief with hunting scenes which are most vividly sculpted.
From Tusculum come the five superb mosaics dating from the 3rd and 4th centuries, set into the floor of the entrance room and depicting hunting scenes and gladiators fighting with wild beasts.
There are four more Roman mosaics in the floor of Room VII, three with masked figures, and the fourth, an extremely interesting work, depicting the federal rites of the ancient Italic peoples.

BAROQUE AND NEOCLASSICAL SCULPTURE

Scipione Borghese was not only consumed by a love of art and of collecting works of art which led him to search out paintings by famous artists and classical works; he also had an innate and indisputable gift for discovering new talent, whose best work he snapped up himself. Thus Cardinal Scipione played the role of Maecenas to the young Gian Lorenzo Bernini, from whom he commissioned some of the artist's best sculptures, which now form the glory of the Borghese Museum. It is certain that the first work to leave the hands of the young Bernini, just seventeen years old, was the charming sculpture of Jupiter with a little faun being suckled by the she-goat Amalthea, in which the artist shows a precocious maturity in the way in which he develops a Hellenistic theme and in his mastery of technical skill.

The Rape of Proserpina is dated 1622, and here the genius of Bernini seems still to be under the influence of the somewhat cold academic style of his father's works. However his innovative gifts are already to be seen in the realism of the weeping Proserpina, in her writhing body and the horrifying figure of Cerberus, the threeheaded-dog, who represents the underworld and the tragic destiny of the abducted girl.

Bernini seems to have reached full artistic maturity with his statue of David, carried out between 1623 and 1624. Its feeling of strength and movement seem to separate it from everything that had gone before, and it is one of the high points of the new Baroque style. In the beautiful face, tensed with the effort and concentration of the moment just before he casts the stone that is to kill Goliath, Bernini has given

Gian Lorenzo Bernini: small bust of Paul V (1612-1622). Room XIV.

Jupiter with a small faun suckled by the She-Goat Amalthea, Bernini's first work (1615). Room XIV.

Bernini: the two busts of Scipione Borghese (1625). Room XIV.

◄ **Bernini: Youthful self-portrait (c. 1623). Room XV.**

Pietro Bernini (1563-1629): Aeneas and Anchises. ► **Room VI.**

us a portrait of his own features. In the sculpture of Apollo and Daphne, made in 1624, the feeling of movement is softened by the poetry and emotion that pervade this work. The artist has caught the climax of the story, the most dramatic moment when Apollo has reached the nymph Daphne after a long chase, but she is already turning into a laurel tree. The god's amazement is contrasted with the almost bloodcurdling cry of Daphne, which brings home the full effect of her metamorphosis.
In about 1625 Bernini carried out the two busts of his great patron, Cardinal

15

Bernini: David (1623-4). Room II.

16

Detail of Bernini's David.

Bernini: Apollo and Daphne (1624). Room III.

18

Daphne: detail.

◀ Bernini: The Rape of Proserpina (1622). Room II.

Bernini: Truth (1645). Room VI.

Bernini: model for the equestrian statue of Louis XIV (c. 1678). Room XIV.

Scipione Borghese. When the artist was working on the first of these two portraits and the work was almost finished, a vein appeared in the marble, running right across the Cardinal's brow. Bernini then executed a second bust in the space of two weeks, exactly similar to the first one, though with less feeling and spontaneity.

In Room XIV, as well as the She-Goat Amalthea and the busts of Cardinal Borghese, there are two more works by Bernini — a small bust of Pope Paul V and a terracotta model for an equestrian statue of Louis XIV of France. The final two works in the collection of sculpture by Bernini are a small bronze of Neptune in Room IV and « Truth », begun in 1645, in Room VI. The Museum also contains other modern sculpture, including the 18 busts of Roman emperors in porphyry and alabaster in the fourth room, the vases of the Seasons by Labourer and the Sleeping Cupid by Algardi. One of the most famous masterpieces is a work of the early 19th century, the sculpture of Pauline Borghese as Venus. This was a potrait by Canova of the young sister of Napoleon Bonaparte, the wife of Camillo Borghese. The artist has managed to trascend the cold perfection of the neoclassical style in the natural grace of this figure.

Canova: Pauline Borghese Bonaparte as Venus (1805). Room I.

24

RENAISSANCE PAINTINGS

The rarity and great value of the collection of Renaissance paintings is also due to the enterprise and power of Cardinal Scipione, who as nephew of the Pope usually managed to get whatever he wanted. This was how he gained possession, for example, of Raphael's Deposition, moved at dead of night from the Baglioni Chapel in the Church of St. Francis in Perugia by the Franciscan Fathers themselves. He also received two of Paolo Veronese's greatest works as a gift from the Patriarch of Aquileia, the *Sermon of St. John the Baptist* and *St. Anthony Preaching to the Fishes*. Even the powerful Cardinal Sfondrato was compelled to sell him 70 pictures, including two masterpieces by Titian, *Sacred and Profane Love* and *Venus Blindfolding Love.* The Gallery also contains valuable works of the 15th century, such as the enigmatic *Portrait of a Man* by Antonello da Messina and the lovely *Madonna and Child with St. John and Angels* by Botticelli, in which the figures are bathed in a

◀ Antonio Canova: Pauline Borghese Bonaparte as Venus (1805), detail. Room I.

Antonello da Messina: Portrait of a Man (c. 1473). Room XX.

Botticelli (1445-1510) and assistants: Madonna with Child, St. John and Angels. Room IX.

Lorenzo di Credi (1459-1537): Virgin with Child and S. Giovannino. Room IX.

Perugino (1450-1523): Madonna and Child. Room IX.

Pinturicchio (1454-1513): Crucifixion with St. Jerome and St. Christopher. Room IX.

◄ Raphael (1483-1520): Portrait of a Young Woman with a Unicorn.

Raphael: Portrait of a Man. Room IX.

Raphael: The Deposition (1507). Room IX.

light which dissolves into soft, delicate colours, harmoniously flowing round the circular shape of the picture without creating any harsh effect. Another superb round picture hangs in the same room as the Botticelli, and highlights the difference in concept between two works by near-contemporaries. This is the *Madonna and Child* by Lorenzo di Credi, in which the central axis of the pyramidal composition is emphasized; its apex is the gentle face of the Virgin, and in the background there is a tranquil landscape in the Flemish style. The Umbrian school, represented by Perugino's *Madonna and Child* and a finely-drawn *Crucifixion* by Pinturicchio, reaches its highest point here with three works by Raphael. They are the *Deposition*, already mentioned, a vigorous *Portrait of a Man* and a delicate *Portrait of a Young Woman with a Unicorn,* only recently attributed to the great painter of Urbino, after restoration revealed

Girolamo Savoldo (c. 1480-1548): Tobias and the Angel. Room XI.

Lucas Cranach (1472-1533): Venus and Cupid with a Honeycomb. Room X.

Andrea del Brescianino (active between 1507 and 1525): Venus with two cupids. Room X.

Copy of Leonardo's Leda.

Correggio (1494-1534): Danae. Room XIX.

that it had been painted over to represent St. Catherine.

The intense introspection of these two portraits contrasts with the dramatic tension of the Deposition, pervaded as it is by emotion and grief at the death of Christ. This work clearly reveals the influence of Michelangelo on Raphael, especially in the figure of Christ, which echoes that in the Pietà in St. Peter's, and the kneeling woman who supports the fainting Virgin (compare the Doni Madonna).

A more recent acquisition by the gallery, bought in 1808 for ten thousand lire, is *Tobias and the Angel* by Girolamo Savoldo, who is also represented by two other works, a *Study* for a portrait and the *Sleeping Venus*.

That Cardinal Borghese was not merely a collector of great good taste, but also had an exceptionally open-minded ap-

38

proach to art, is clearly demonstrated by the painting by Luca Cranach of *Venus and Cupid holding a Honeycomb,* whose cold northern charm stands out markedly from the other works in the gallery. One need only compare it with the warm classical style of Andrea del Brescianino's *Venus,* in which the cleverly-used play of light gives a three-dimensional effect.

What is perhaps Correggio's most famous masterpiece, *Danae*, was not acquired by the Borghese family until 1823, after it had travelled round various cities in Europe. The intense poetry of this work lies not only in the warm caressing colour that pervades it, but is transmuted into the classical myth, whose true essence is clearl perceived and yet interpreted in a modern spirit. Venetian painting is well represented by the works of the leading artists of

◄ **Giovanni Bellini: Madonna and Child (1505-10). Room XX.**

Lorenzo Lotto: Virgin and Child with Saints (1508). Room XI.

40

Titian: Sacred and Profane Love (c. 1512). Room XX.

Titian: Sacred and Profane Love (c. 1512), detail. Room XX.

Titian: Venus Blindfolding Love (1565). Room XX.

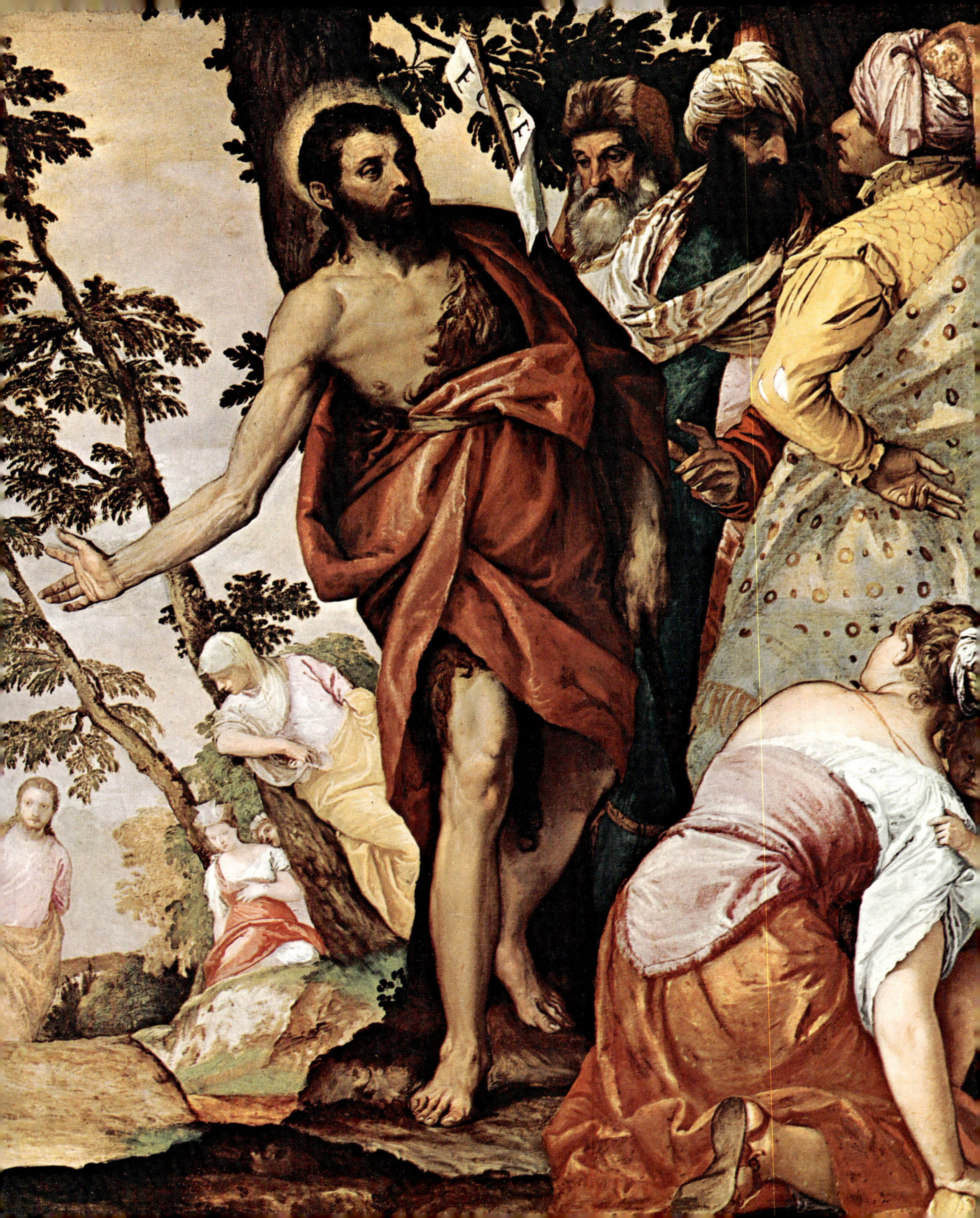
ECCE

◀ Veronese (1528-88): The Sermon of St. John the Baptist. Room XX.

Veronese (1528-88): St. Anthony Preaching to the Fishes. Room XX.

this school – the calm beauty of Giovanni Bellini's *Madonna,* Lorenzo Lotto's *Virgin and Child with Saints,* which shows the influence of Dürer, and works by Titian, Veronese and Jacopo Bassano.

The four works by Titian in the gallery enable us to follow the development of the master's artistic style, from the profound, serene lyricism of the perfectly-drawn figures of *Sacred and Profane Love* to the pictures in which form dissolves into pure colour – *Venus Blindfolding Love, St. Dominic* and the *Flagellation of Christ.* Titian achieves form by means of the intense use of colour tones, and for this reason he painted on large convases, using various depths of colour and thicknesses of paint. His figures are not painted in detail, they are created by means of light and colour. This is a characteristic that appears with increasing frequency in his later work.

Jacopo Bassano (1516-92): The Last Supper. Room XVI.

The two works by Veronese, the *Sermon of St. John the Baptist* and *St. Anthony Preaching to the Fishes*, represent the high point of decorative art, and demonstrate the artist's leaning towards an extreme refinement that often carries echoes of oriental motifs interpreted in a classical manner.

Of the works by Dosso Dossi sent to Scipione Borghese from Ferrara, perhaps the most outstanding is *Circe*, a superb painting that is full of fascination and mystery.

Other important works are Andrea del Sarto's *Pietà* and *Madonna with Child*, and Angelo Bronzino's monumental *St. John the Baptist*.

Dosso Dossi (1489-1542): Circe. Room XIX.

46

BAROQUE PAINTINGS

Perhaps the most interesting group of works in the gallery consists of the 17th century paintings. This we owe to the discernment of Scipione Borghese, who had the wit to snap up no less than eight pictures by a young artist who had an extremely bad reputation at the papal court, but whose greatness and highly innovative gifts the cardinal was among the first to recognize: Michelangelo Merisi, known to us as Caravaggio. Thus Cardinal Borghese acquired the huge canvas of the *Madonna of the Palafrenieri* after 1605; it had been painted for one of the altars in St. Peter's, but was rejected by the Cardinals at the Vatican because they considered it unsuitable for a holy place. It is indeed a truly revolutionary work, not only because of the power

◄ Andrea del Sarto: Madonna and Child with St. John (c. 1514). Room X.

Caravaggio (1573-1610): St. Jerome. Room XIV.

48

◄ Bronzino (1503-72): St. John the Baptist. Room X.   Caravaggio (1573-1610): St. John the Baptist in the Wilderness.

50

◄ Caravaggio (1573-1610): The Young Bacchus, III. Room XIV.

Caravaggio (1573-1610): St. John the Baptist in the Wilderness.

52

53

◂ Caravaggio: The Madonna of the Palafrenieri (1605). Room XIV.

Caravaggio (1573-1610): David with the Head of Goliath. Room XIV.

Guercino (1591-1666): The Return of the Prodigal Son. Room XIV.

that the contrast of light and shade gives to the picture, but also because of the realism and uninhibitedly natural style in which it is painted.

After they had been confiscated for the non-payment of taxes from the studio of the Cavalier d'Arpino, two more paintings by Caravaggio were added to the collection in 1607 – the *Young Bacchus, III,* and *Boy with a Basket of Fruit.* These were painted when the artist was very young, just after his arrival in Rome. Some people believe that the Young Bacchus is a self-portrait of Caravaggio when he was recovering from Malaria.

Later Scipione Borghese bought other paintings from the artist himself – St. Jerome, in which the use of light plays an even more important part in the construction of the picture, St. John the Baptist in the Desert, David with the Head of Goliath, whose dramatic quality is heightened by the melancholy expression on the face of the young hero, a portrait of Paul V which is now lost, and the very famous *Supper at Emmaus,* now in the National Gallery in London.

Gherardo Honthorst (1592-1662): Concert. Room VIII.

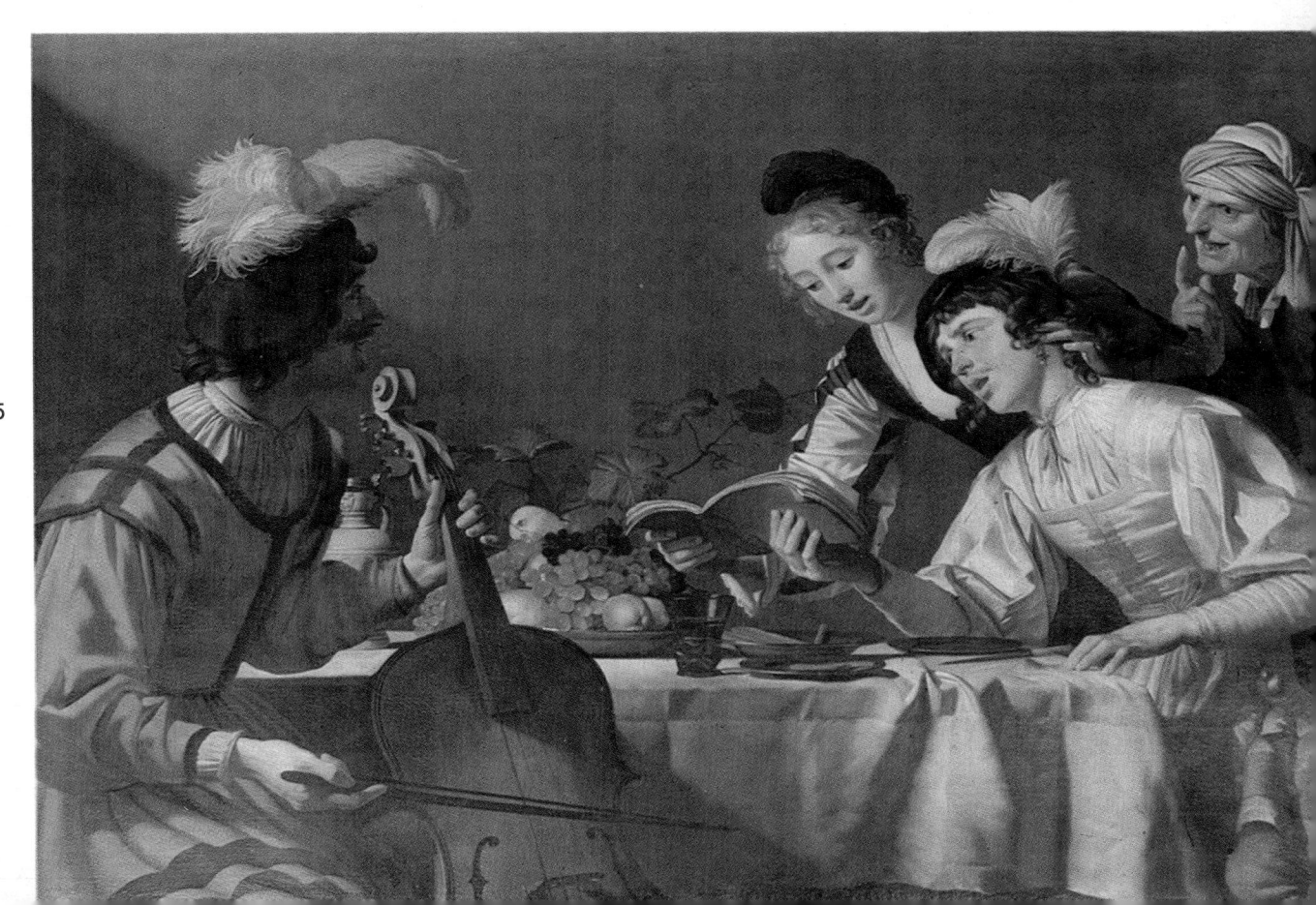

Domenichino (1581-1641): The Sybil. Room XII.

Domenichino (1581-1641): Diana the Huntress. Room XIV.

The art of the 17th century is represented here by more conventional painters as well, such as Guercino (*Samson holding out the Honeycomb to his Parents* and *The Return of the Prodigal Son*), Gherardo Honthorst, known as Gherardo delle Notti, who uses light in the manner of Caravaggio, so that it falls on the figures in such a way as to highlight the refinement of the decoration; and Domenichino. From him the Cardinal commissioned the painting of the *Sybil*, which reveals the artist's intense love of colour in the beautiful skin tones of the face and the rich garments, and *Diana Hunting*, one of Domenichino's best works, full of charm and fascination.

Other paintings worthy of note are those by Sassoferrato and Pompeo Batoni's *Madonna with Child*, full of eighteenth century charm.

There are also two works by Rubens, painted during his visits to Rome: *Susanna and the Elders* and the *Deposition*.

58

◂ Sassoferrato (1609-85): Madonna and Child. Room XII.

Pompeo Batoni (1708-87): Madonna and Child. Room XII.

Peter Paul Rubens: The Deposition of Christ (c. 1605). Room XV.

Funerary urn in red porphyry, from the Mausoleum of Hadrian. Room IV.

THE MARBLES

In order that the Casino Borghese might fulfil its purpose as a museum to the full, Cardinal Scipione directed that the decoration of the interior should be limited to marble columns and the borders that frame the doors and windows, so that the visitor's attention would be focused on the wonderful collection of sculpture that constitutes the true ornamentation of the Villa.

When in the 18th century Asprucci supervised the renovation of the Villa at the wish of Marcantonio Borghese, he not only devised a series of frescoes whose subject-matter was inspired by the works housed in the various rooms, but also called on the services of skilled sculptors of marble, whose masterpieces are to be found in the room at the back of the ground-floor, known as the Hall of the Emperors. This represents the high point of the refinement and polychromy that are typical of the eighteenth century. The walls, which are decorated with mosaics, ornamentation in cipollino, jasper, antique yellow and alabaster, and niches containing statues, are divided up by alabaster pilasters whose capitals are of gilded metal. In the centre of each pilaster there is a hexagonal medallion in Lunigiana marble with a blue mosaic background, the work of Pietro Rudiez, while the floor is made up of squares of marble of different types and colours. The richness and variety of the decoration is enhanced by the two huge tables in red porphyry with winged lions in Moricone alabaster, the two columns in oriental alabaster that flank one of the doors, the 18 busts of Roman emperors in porphyry and alabaster, two tables in porphyry with bases in rare marbles, the four vases in Lunigiana marble by Massimiliano Laboureur, representing the Seasons, vases and urns in antique black, vases and bowls in porphyry and the huge funerary urn in red porphyry that came from Hadrian's Mausoleum.

INDEX TO ILLUSTRATIONS

Andrea del Brescianino - Venus with Two Cupids	35
Andrea del Sarto - Madonna and Child with St. John.	46
Antonello da Messina - Portrait of a man	25
Archaic Greek Art - Statue of a Girl	9
Asprucci Antonio - Fountain of Aesculapius	4
Hall of the Emperors	7
Asprucci Mario - Temple of Aesculapius in the Garden of the Lake	5
Bassano Jacopo - The Last Supper	44
Batoni Pompeo - Madonna and Child	59
Bellini Giovanni - Madonna and Child	38
Bernini Gian Lorenzo - Small bust of Paul V	13
Jupiter and Faun Suckled by the Goat Amalthea	13
Two portraits of Scipione Borghese	14
Youthful Self-portrait	14
David	16
David (detail)	17
Apollo and Daphne	18
Apollo and Daphne (detail)	19
Rape of Proserpina	20
Model for the equestrian statue of Louis XIV	21
Truth	22
Bernini Pietro - Aeneas and Anchises	15
Botticelli Sandro and assistants - Madonna and Child, St. John and Angels	26
Bronzino - St. John the Baptist	47
Calandra-Rubino - Equestrian statue of Umberto I	8
Canina Luigi - The Propyleae at the entrance in Piazzale Flaminia	3
Canova Antonio - Pauline Borghese Bonaparte (detail)	23
Pauline Borghese Bonaparte	24
Caravaggio - St. Jerome	48
Boy with a Basket of Fruit	49
The Young Bacchus, Ill.	50
St. John the Baptist in the Wilderness	51
Madonna of the Palafrenieri	52
David with the head of Goliath	53
Correggio - Danae	37
Cranach Lucas - Venus and Cupid with a Honeycomb	34
Domenichino - The Sybil	56
Diana the Huntress	57
Dossi Dosso - Circe	45
Eberlein Gustavo - Statue of Goethe	8
Facade of Casino Borghese (rear)	64
Facade of Casino Borghese (main)	6
Greek Art, 3rd century - Dancing Satyr	9
Guercino - The Return of the Prodigal Son	54
Honthorst Gherardo - Concert	55
Leonardo (copy)	36
Lotto Lorenzo - Virgin and Child with Saints	39
Lorenzo di Credi - Madonna and Child with St. John	27
Perugino - Madonna and Child	28
Pinturicchio - Crucifixion with St. Jerome and St. Christopher	29
Rainaldi Girolamo - The Aviaries	6
Raphael - Portrait of a Young Woman with a Unicorn	30
Portrait of a Man	31
The Deposition	32
Roman Art - Boy on a Dolphin	10
Leda and the Swan	11
Mosaic with gladiators fighting	12
Urn in porphyry from the Mausoleum of Hadrian	61
Rubens Peter Paul - The Deposition of Christ	60
Savoldo Girolamo - Tobias and the Angel	33
Sassoferrato - Madonna and Child	58
Titian - Sacred and Profane Love (detail)	40
Sacred and Profane Love	41
Venus Blindfolding Love	41
Thorwaldsen Alberto (copy) - Statue of Byron	8
Unterberger Cristoforo - Fountain of the Seahorses	4
Veronese Paolo - Sermon of St. John the Baptist	42
St. Anthony Preaching to the Fishes	43

Rear facade of the Casino Borghese.